Simply Delicious

DESSERT

Nancy Schechtman

Copyright © 2015 Nancy Schechtman
All rights reserved.

ISBN: 1514857510
ISBN 13: 9781514857519

Introduction

I don't know when my passion to bake began or where it came from. I would guess that it started with Toll House Cookies, like so many others, and grew into a profession.

My first venture into catering was selling "Gooey" brownies to neighboring pizza places. When I expanded the business, only appetizers and desserts were on the menu. The principle is that if you wow your guests with their first bite and the lingering memory is of a fabulous sweet concoction, then it hardly matters what you make and serve in the middle. It is one of the great secrets of easy entertaining!

These recipes are simple and delicious just as in Simply Delicious Appetizers cookbook. Some cakes have more steps and require patience but the end result for these is well worth the time and effort. Clear directions make it easy for you to please your family and guests.

World's Largest Chocolate Fountain
Bellagio Hotel, Las Vegas

Dedication

To my Cookie Monsters
Keri, Kenny, Bill and Sue

To Marty
Who can find chocolate in the deepest recesses of the freezer

Multi-tasking one afternoon at home; plum galette, brownies, chocolate chip cookies, Nancy's chocolate cake and pasta for supper.

Table of Contents

Baking Tips · viii

Baking Staples · xi

Cookies · 1

Brownies & Bars · 17

Cake · 31

Desserts · 47

Ice Cream Pie with Variations · 61

Conversion Table · 64

Interesting Information · 65

Index · 67

Thank You · 71

Baking Tips

- Ensure baking ingredients are at room temperature before beginning. Butter and eggs are safe at room temperature for several hours.
- Butter cannot be overbeaten. The texture should be very creamy.
- Use unsalted butter when baking for flavor. The salt content in "sweetened butter" varies drastically between manufacturers. Better to just add the amount suggested in the recipe. Salt, though not a leavening agent, provides stability during the rising process.
- 2% milk can be used rather than whole milk but skimmed milk does not have enough fat for a moist product.
- Have two measuring cups on hand, one each for wet and dry ingredients.
- Combine all dry ingredients before adding any liquids, including eggs, so that the chemical reaction with baking powder, for example, does not begin prematurely. And, you want to be certain that dry additions to flour are fully incorporated.
- When a recipe says to scrape sides of bowl, be certain to also scrape the bottom.
- When measuring brown and granulated sugars, pack brown sugar into measuring cup then pour granulated on top. You will end up with the exact amount of the total.
- I always use large eggs versus regular sized. Your pastry will be moister.
- I do not own a flour sifter. I use different size sieves. Instead of cranking you just tap the side of the sieve; much easier with the same result.
- Instead of buying expensive pastry brushes, use paint brushes with melted butter and frosting. They spread more evenly than silicone brushes.
- Lavender is a lovely addition to anything with fruit, especially lemon, as it heightens the flavor and provides a beautiful balance. There are many places online to purchase home grown lavender.
- Before squeezing a lemon, roll it on your counter to get more juice.
- When whipping cream have everything cold; cream, beaters and bowl. I put the beaters and bowl in the freezer for 10-30 minutes.
- To hold whipped cream for several hours place in cold bowl lined with cheesecloth and refrigerate.
- Whipping cream from a can should never be used in baking. Only home whipped cream beaten on a medium speed with patience and an ever moving wrist produces whipping cream worthy of your efforts.

- As egg whites can expand eightfold during the whipping process, use a large bowl.
- The bowl and whisk or beater must be completely free of grease of the whites will not whip.
- Do not separate eggs over the bowl as the tiniest bit of yolk will prevent the whites from expanding.
- The cap on a bottle of vanilla measures 1 teaspoon.
- When melting chocolate in the microwave, use 1 minute increments, stirring well each time you check its progress. It is better to not melt entirely. Stir with a wooden spoon until smooth.
- For chocolate glaze melt 2 ounces chocolate with 4 tablespoons unsalted butter.
- Most people forget about the food processor when baking. I use mine often and there are several recipes in the book that demonstrate how a processor can save time and perform a task more simply.
- I always line cookie sheets with parchment. Pull the whole sheet off the pan after baking with the cookies on it and you will not need to cool them on racks.
- All of these recipes can be doubled with no worries. Cookies can be tripled if your mixer will hold the quantity of ingredient.

Kitchen near Cusco, Peru

Baking Staples

Granulated, Brown and Confectioner's Sugar
Unbleached Flour
Baking Powder
Baking Soda
Cornstarch
Vanilla Extract
Unsweetened Cocoa Powder
Chocolate: Semi-sweet, Sweet, Bittersweet, Unsweetened
Chocolate Chips
Coconut
Shortening Spray
Honey

Corn Syrup
Molasses
Allspice
Cardamom
Ground Cinnamon, Cinnamon Sticks
Ground Cloves
Ground Ginger
Dried Lavender
Ground Nutmeg
Salt
Unsalted Butter
Eggs
Fresh Lemon Juice and Lime Juice

Equipment

Stand Mixer
Nesting Bowls
Whisks in various sizes
Several Spatulas
Sieves
Colanders
Scale
Paint Brushes
Citrus Reamer

Batter Scoops
Doilies
Muffin Cups
Ruler
Parchment
Food Processor
Zester
Microplane

I started making Toll House cookies for Sue and Bill on their first visit 18 years ago. I can't begin to count how many have been consumed in the intervening years.

Cookies

"Me want cookie!" Cookie Monster
Cookies are as fun to bake as they are to eat and make the whole house smell wonderful. They are also a super family project, a good time to share with your kids and their friends and an opportunity to teach fractions. As much as you have been told to be exact when baking, cookies are a good way to experiment a bit with your own favorite flavors by substituting candies for chips, almond extract for vanilla or adding espresso.

Luscious Sugar Cookies   Makes 36

These were a big seller at the store. They can be made any size and decorated should you choose. The lemon is what makes them irresistible and a pinch of dried lavender makes them out-of-this world!

1 cup unsalted butter
1 cup sugar
½ cup packed brown sugar
2 large egg yolks
1/8 teaspoon nutmeg
Grated rind of one lemon or lime

Juice of one lemon or lime
2 teaspoons vanilla extract
2 1/2 cups unbleached flour
2 teaspoons baking powder
1 teaspoon dried lavender, optional
3/4 teaspoon salt

Preheat oven to 400'.
Grease two baking sheets lightly or line with parchment. Cream butter until soft and creamy. Gradually add sugars, beat until fluffy. Add egg yolks one at a time beating well after each addition. Blend in lemon rind, juice and vanilla. Sift together flour, baking powder and salt; stir into dough. Add lavender and nutmeg. If dough seems too dry, add water 1 teaspoon at a time. Scoop dough into balls, place on baking sheets. Using a glass with a bottom about the size of the cookies, dip into sugar, granulated or colored; flatten each cookie   using the bottom of the glass. Keep dipping the glass in sugar as needed so that dough does not stick. Bake   about 6 minutes or until just golden.

SIMPLY DELICIOUS

Chewy Oatmeal Toffee Crunch Cookies   Makes 24
One of my favorite candies comes alive with the texture of oatmeal. You can use any crunchy candy.

¾ cup pecans
¾ cup firmly packed brown sugar
¾ cup unsalted butter
½ cup sugar
1 large egg
1 teaspoon vanilla extract

1½ cups old fashioned oatmeal
1 cup unbleached flour
½ teaspoon baking soda
Pinch salt
1 6-ounce package, 1½ cups, Heath bars, cut into ½-inch pieces

Preheat oven to 350°.
Lightly grease 2 cookie sheets or line with parchment paper. Coarsely chop pecans in processor; set aside. Process sugars, butter, 1/2 cup sugar, egg and vanilla until fluffy, stopping once to scrape down sides of bowl, about 1 minute. Add oats, flour, baking soda and salt; mix until just combined using 2 to 3 on/off turns; do not over process. Transfer to bowl. Stir in pecans and chopped English toffee. Mound dough by ¼ cupfuls onto prepared sheets placing 2 inches apart; flatten slightly using fingers or back of wooden spoon. Bake until dry in appearance and centers are slightly soft to touch, about 20 minutes. Cool on cookie sheets 10 minutes. Transfer to rack; cool completely; store in airtight container.

Walnut Lace Cookies   Makes 60
These small see-through cookies are thin, crisp and delicious. Also try breaking them up to use as topping for ice cream or mixed into salad instead of spiced nuts. Keep broken cookies in an airtight container or in the freezer for future use. Butter can be frozen and shaved to help incorporate.

1/3 cup unbleached flour
½ teaspoon baking powder
Pinch salt
¼ cup unsalted butter

1 cup firmly packed brown sugar
1 large egg
1 cup chopped walnuts

Preheat oven to 375°.
Grease cookie sheets or line with parchment paper. Sift together flour, baking powder and salt. Blend butter, brown sugar and dry ingredients with pastry blender as for pie crust. Add egg, mix thoroughly; stir in walnuts. Drop by teaspoonfuls about 2 inches apart on cookie sheets. Bake 5 to 6 minutes. Remove from baking sheets at once; cool on racks.

Island Treasure Cookies   Makes 12
Macadamia nuts and coconut, gifts from Hawaii, are truly treasures. For a change of pace, toast both the macadamias and coconut.

1½ cups unbleached flour
2 tablespoons unbleached flour
¾ teaspoon baking powder
¾ teaspoon salt
½ teaspoon baking soda
¾ cup unsalted butter
¾ cup packed brown sugar

1/3 cup sugar
¾ teaspoon vanilla extract
1 large egg
¾ cup coconut
¾ cup chopped macadamia nuts
1½ cups chocolate chunks

Preheat oven to 375°.
Combine flour, baking powder, salt and baking soda. Beat butter until soft; add sugars and vanilla, beat until very creamy. Add egg, mix well. Gradually add flour mixture. Stir in coconut, nuts and chocolate chunks. Drop by rounded tablespoon onto ungreased cookie sheet. Bake 10 to 12 minutes. Let stand for 2 minutes. Move to wire racks to cool completely.

Triple Chocolate Cookies

Makes 48

As if double chocolate wouldn't be enough, these cookies are crispy outside, fudgy within and yummy all the way through.

14 ounces coarsely chopped semi-sweet chocolate chips
5 ounces coarsely chopped unsweetened chocolate
6 tablespoons unsalted butter
1½ cups unbleached flour
¾ teaspoon baking powder
½ teaspoon salt

2 cups sugar
6 large eggs
1 tablespoon strong brewed coffee , optional
1½ teaspoons vanilla extract, use 1 tablespoon if not using coffee
8 ounces coarsely chopped semi-sweet chocolate chips
¾ cup chopped walnuts, optional

Preheat oven to 350°.
Line baking sheets with parchment. Melt 14 ounces semi-sweet chocolate, unsweetened chocolate and butter, stir until smooth. Combine flour, baking powder and salt. Beat sugar and eggs until slowly dissolving ribbon forms when beaters are lifted. Blend in chocolate mixture, coffee and vanilla. Fold in dry ingredients. Stir in remaining chocolate and walnuts. Drop batter by heaping tablespoons onto cookie sheets spacing evenly. Bake until tops are cracked, slightly shiny and soft to touch, about 15 minutes. Cool cookies on baking sheets.

Apricot Buttons Makes 36

A wonderful alternative to chocolate (did I say that?). The buttons look beautiful on a pastry tray for a dessert buffet. Feel free to substitute your favorite jam.

½ pound unsalted butter
¾ cup sugar
2 large eggs separated
1 teaspoon vanilla extract

2 cups unbleached flour
½ teaspoon salt
1½ cups finely ground walnuts
½ cup apricot jam

Preheat oven to 325°.
Grease cookie sheets or line with parchment paper. Beat butter and sugar until smooth. Add egg yolks and vanilla; beat until well blended. Stir in flour and salt; beat just until dough comes together. In a separate bowl, beat egg whites to blend. Place walnuts in a shallow bowl. Shape dough into 1-inch balls. Dip each in egg whites, turning to coat completely; roll in walnuts to coat. Place about 1 inch apart on cookie sheets. Press your thumb gently into center of each cookie to make an imprint. Bake cookies until lightly browned, 18 to 20 minutes. If baking 2 sheets at once, switch their positions halfway through baking. Allow cookies to cool on sheets for 5 minutes. Using a wide spatula, transfer to racks to cool completely. Spoon ½ teaspoon jam into center of each cookie.

Lemon Thumbprint Cookies   Makes 36

Raspberry jelly is equally good or maybe plum, strawberry or another of your personal favorites, including lemon curd. A pinch of lavender added with the lemon zest will intensify the flavors.

1 cup unsalted butter
½ cup sugar
2 large egg yolks
3 tablespoons grated lemon peel
1 tablespoon fresh lemon juice

¼ teaspoon salt
2½ cups unbleached flour
6 tablespoons apricot preserves
Pinch of lavender, optional

Preheat oven to 350°.
Lightly grease baking sheets or line with parchment paper. Beat butter and sugar until well blended. Beat in egg yolks, lemon peel, lemon juice, lavender and salt. Add flour in 2 additions; beat just until moist clumps form. Gather dough together to bind; form into 1-inch balls. Place balls on prepared baking sheets spacing 1 inch apart. Indent center of each ball by pressing firmly with your thumb. Bake cookies until firm to touch and golden brown on bottom, about 22 minutes. Remove from oven. Immediately fill thumbprint with scant ½ teaspoon jam or jelly. Cool completely on racks.

Hazelnut-Cinnamon Biscotti   Makes 32

These are even better when spread with melted chocolate. Peeled hazelnuts are becoming more difficult to find and are expensive but, if you can, they do save time. To peel, toast hazelnuts in 400° oven or in microwave until peels start to crack. Remove from oven, roll between your hands to remove peel, these can be very hot so use of mitts or gloves is wise. Filberts make for a good alternative.

3 cups unbleached flour
1 tablespoon baking powder
½ teaspoon salt
¼ teaspoon ground cinnamon
1 cup toasted, husked hazelnuts

¾ cup sugar
½ cup unsalted butter
1 tablespoon grated orange peel
1 teaspoon vanilla extract
3 large eggs

Preheat oven to 350°.

Grease large baking sheet or line with parchment. Mix flour, baking powder, salt and cinnamon. Coarsely chop hazelnuts in processor. Put aside. Combine sugar and butter in processor; blend until fluffy. Add orange peel and vanilla; blend well. Add eggs one at a time, blending just until incorporated after each addition. Add flour mixture; mix using on/off pulse until just blended; add hazelnuts, process until just blended. Turn dough onto floured work surface; divide in half. Roll each half into 9-inch long, 2-inch wide log; space 3 inches apart of baking sheet. Flatten each to 12-inches long and 2½-inch wide log. Bake until very light golden and firm, about 25 minutes. Cool on baking sheet 5 minutes maintaining oven temperature. Use long metal spatula to transfer logs to work surface. Use serrated knife to cut logs diagonally into ¾-inch wide slice; place slices, cut side down, on baking sheet. Bake 15 minutes; turn biscotti over; bake until light golden and firm, about 15 minutes. Do not over-bake; remove from oven before they look quite done. If biscotti dry out, they will become too hard to bite and will crumble. Cool on racks. Brush with melted chocolate if desired.

Pistachio-Currant Biscotti   Makes 40

I've messed up many biscotti recipes. They became my nemesis until I came up with these that are irresistible. Everyone loves them all day long. There are a few places where you can find the pistachios shelled; they are more expensive but save hours of your time. Try Trader Joe's or Costco. The grated butter technique is one I learned from my daughter-in-law Stacy who makes the best biscuits I've ever tasted.

1 cup chopped pistachio nuts
2¾ cups unbleached flour
2 cups sugar divided
½ cup finely ground pistachio nuts
½ cup currants
½ teaspoon salt
1 teaspoon baking powder

3 tablespoons frozen, grated unsalted butter
3 large eggs
3 large egg yolks
1 teaspoon vanilla extract
2 teaspoons ground cinnamon
2 tablespoons melted unsalted butter

Preheat oven to 350°.
Line baking sheet with parchment paper; grease lightly. Combine flour, 1½ cup sugar, ground pistachios, salt and baking powder. Gently mix in butter until crumbly. Whisk together eggs, egg yolks and vanilla. Mix egg mixture into dry ingredients until just combined; stir nuts and currants into mixture. Turn batter onto lightly floured work surface; knead 2 to 3 minutes. Add flour as necessary to make dough easy to handle; divide into 3 balls. Roll each ball out to logs about 10 inches long and 1½-inches wide. Combine remaining ½ cup sugar with cinnamon; roll tops of each log into mixture; place on baking sheet. Bake 30 to 35 minutes until lightly browned and slightly soft to touch. Remove from oven; reduce temperature to 300°. Cool logs 5 minutes. Cut logs into ½ to ¾-inches slices; lay flat on baking sheet. Return to oven; bake additional 10 to 12 minutes until just beginning to brown.

   Cool 10 minutes on baking rack. Brush top side of each piece with melted butter; dip in remaining cinnamon-sugar mixture. Allow to dry 5 minutes. Store in airtight container lined with waxed paper. Will keep several weeks and are fine in the freezer.

NANCY SCHECHTMAN

Coconut Macaroons   Makes 20

Macaroons are so delicious, good any time of year and perfect for Passover and with coffee. For variety add 3 tablespoons of cocoa; 1 cup chocolate chips or both. It is nice to have a variety when serving to company or family and the combination looks nice on a tray. Recipe doubles and triples easily.

3 cups, 8 ounces, shredded coconut
2 teaspoons almond or vanilla extract
Pinch salt

¾ cup sweetened condensed milk
2 large egg whites beaten to stiff peaks

Preheat oven to 350°.
Grease cookie sheets well or line with parchment paper. Mix coconut, vanilla, salt and condensed milk to make thick paste. Fold in egg whites. Form into balls or drop from teaspoon onto cookie sheets about 2 inches apart. Bake 8 to 12 minutes until edges are lightly browned. Store in airtight container.

This lovely lady served us baklava with afternoon coffee in a remote village on Corfu, Greece

Baklava **Makes 16**

Baklava is dessert to us. In Greece it is an afternoon snack served with sweet iced coffee. Try this authentic rendition of the Greek favorite. I keep some in the freezer individually wrapped at all times as this is one of Marty's absolute favorites, he raves about it. Pistachios serve as a substitute for the walnuts.

1½ cups finely chopped walnuts
1 cup chopped almonds
1/3 cup sugar
1 teaspoon ground cinnamon
¼ teaspoon ground cardamom
1/8 teaspoon ground cloves
16 sheets phyllo dough

¾ cup melted unsalted butter
1 cup sugar
1 cup water
1 cup good grade honey
1 3- inch strip lemon peel
½ vanilla bean halved lengthwise
1 cinnamon stick

Preheat oven to 350°.
Lightly butter bottom and sides of 9x13-inch pan with melted butter. Combine walnuts, almonds, 1/3 cup sugar, cinnamon, cardamom and cloves. Using bottom of pan, cut phyllo to fit, discarding any scraps. Place one sheet phyllo into pan, brush lightly with butter. Layer 3 more sheets over first, buttering each; sprinkle 1/3 nut mixture over dough. Layer 4 more sheets of phyllo over nut mixture buttering each one. Sprinkle with 1/3 nut mixture. Repeat. Finish with 4 more sheets buttering each one. Using a sharp knife, score baklava into diamond-shaped pieces by cutting through top layers of phyllo. Bake until crisp and brown, 35 to 45 minutes.

Combine remaining ingredients in large saucepan. Bring to boil over medium-high heat. Reduce heat to low; simmer until it is the consistency of thick maple syrup, about 10 minutes. Remove from heat, cool slightly. Pour ½ the warm syrup over baklava immediately as it comes from oven. Turn pan upside down on rack over foil allowing syrup to drain; cool baklava completely. Serve room temperature or chilled.

Fantasy Fudge Cookies

Makes 60

The fantasy is created by your choice of candy.

1 cup unsalted butter
1½ cups sugar
2 large eggs
1 teaspoon vanilla extract
2 cups unbleached flour

2/3 cup unsweetened cocoa
3/4 cup baking soda
1/2 teaspoon salt
1 8-ounce package Reese's pieces
¼ cup semi-sweet chocolate chips

Preheat oven to 350°.
Lightly grease baking sheets or line with parchment paper. Cream butter with sugar until light; blend in eggs one at a time beating until smooth. Stir in vanilla. Combine flour, cocoa powder, baking soda and salt. Slowly beat into creamed mixture. Stir in candy and chocolate chips. Drop batter by teaspoonfuls onto prepared sheets spacing 2 inches apart. Bake until set but still very soft, 10 to 12 minutes. Cool on racks to completely cool, they will firm as they cool.

Chocolate Mint Sugar Drops

Makes 30

The only place that I can now find chocolate mint chips is online at Hershey's website but it is certainly worth taking the time to obtain them. Do not order during the hot summer months as they can melt in transit. I have just noticed chocolate chips filled with mint in the grocery; these would work, too.

2½ cups unbleached flour
1½ teaspoons baking powder
¾ teaspoon salt
1¼ cups sugar divided

¾ cup canola oil
2 large eggs
1 teaspoon vanilla extract
10 ounces mint chocolate chips

Preheat oven to 350°.
Combine flour, baking powder and salt. Beat together 1 cup sugar and canola oil; mix well. Beat in eggs and vanilla. Gradually add flour mixture; stir in mint chocolate chips. Drop by rounded teaspoonfuls onto ungreased cookie sheets. Shape into balls; roll balls in remaining sugar. Bake 12 minutes until lightly crackled. Cool but they are wonderful eaten warm.

White Chocolate Haystacks Makes 32

Very simple, very addicting, these are a terrific addition to your Christmas collection. You can also drizzle the haystacks with melted dark or semi-sweet chocolate. It makes for a lovely presentation to have both.

12 ounces chopped, white chocolate
1½ cups salted Spanish peanuts, with skins
1½ cups thin pretzel sticks, broken into 1½-inch pieces

Line baking sheet with waxed paper. Melt chocolate in top of double boiler over barely simmering water, stirring until smooth and creamy. Add nuts and pretzels, stirring until well coated with chocolate. Remove pan from heat; spoon mixture by rounded teaspoonfuls onto baking sheet. Cool to room temperature or refrigerate to set chocolate. These can be kept indefinitely in the refrigerator if they last that long.

Decadent Peanut Butter Chocolate Chunk Cookies Makes 36

The word decadent says it all! Plan ahead, this dough needs 3 hours of refrigeration before baking.

1 16-ounce jar creamy peanut butter
½ cup unsalted butter
2½ cups firmly packed brown sugar
3 large eggs
1 tablespoon vanilla extract
1½ cups unbleached flour
2½ teaspoons baking powder
½ teaspoon salt
1½ cups chopped roasted peanuts
2 cups chocolate chunks

Preheat oven to 325°.
Grease cookie sheets or line with parchment paper. Beat peanut butter and butter until very creamy; gradually beat in brown sugar. Add eggs one at a time beating well after each addition; beat in vanilla. Mix flour, baking powder and salt; add to peanut butter mixture, stir until just combined. Mix in chopped peanuts and chocolate chunks. Cover and refrigerate dough until well chilled, about 3 hours. Shape dough into 1-inch diameter balls; place on prepared cookie sheets spacing 2 inches apart. Bake until tops of cookies are light brown and dry to the touch, about 12 minutes. Cool on cookie sheets 5 minutes; cool completely on racks.

Mint Chocolate Cookies Makes 36

Here we go again with mint. You could easily substitute almond extract or brewed espresso for the peppermint. It is that easy to alter a recipe, even with baked goods.

1 cup unsalted butter
1¾ cups sugar
2 large eggs
¾ teaspoon peppermint extract
2 cups unbleached flour

1 cup unsweetened cocoa
1 teaspoon baking soda
½ teaspoon baking powder
½ teaspoon salt

Preheat oven to 350°.
Line two baking sheets with parchment paper. Beat butter and sugar until well blended; add eggs and peppermint extract. Add dry ingredients; beat until well blended. Form dough into 1-inch balls; place 2 inches apart on baking sheets. Flatten balls slightly to 1½-inch rounds. Bake cookies until edges begin to firm but center still appears soft and top is crackled, about 13 to 15 minutes. Cool on baking sheets 5 minutes. Transfer cookies to racks to cool completely.

Chocolate-Filled Thumbprint Cookies   Makes 36

These require time to prepare but are definitely worth that time and will disappear quickly. They are a favorite of my high school students, especially when I challenge them to make each of their batches consistent with the other students'.

1 cup unsalted butter
1 cup packed brown sugar
2 teaspoons vanilla extract
3 cups sifted unbleached flour
½ cup semi-sweet chocolate chips
2 tablespoons milk
½ teaspoon salt

½ cup confectioners' sugar
1¾ cups semi-sweet chocolate chips
2 tablespoons solid shortening
¼ cup light corn syrup
2 tablespoons water
1 teaspoon vanilla

Preheat oven to 350°.
Blend butter, brown sugar and vanilla until creamy. Stir in flour, chocolate chips, milk and salt; mix well; use extra milk if dough is crumbly. Form dough into 1-inch balls; arrange on ungreased baking sheets. Indent center of each ball by pressing firmly with your thumb. Bake cookies 12 to 15 minutes or until golden brown. Immediately roll in confectioners' sugar covering completely. Cool completely on racks. Melt chocolate and shortening in double boiler over simmering water or in microwave; remove from heat. Stir in remaining ingredients until mixture is smooth. Cool 5 minutes. Place generous ½ teaspoon filling in each thumbprint. Store in airtight container.

Brownies & Bars

I have yet to meet a person who doesn't like some kind of brownie, they are just that irresistible. My very first foray into the world of catering was selling my Gooey brownies to pizza places. I owe a lifetime in the world of food to a brownie.

OMG Brownies   Makes 16
I always double this recipe because one never lasts long enough.

¾ cup unbleached flour
¾ cup unsweetened cocoa
¼ tablespoon salt
½ cup unsalted butter
½ cup sugar
½ cup packed brown sugar

3 large eggs
1 tablespoon vanilla extract
1 cup chopped pecans
¾ cup white chocolate chips
½ cup caramel ice cream topping
¾ cup semisweet chocolate chips

Preheat oven to 350°.
Grease 8-inch square pan, line with foil with ends overlapping the pan. Sift together cocoa, flour and salt set aside. Beat butter until light; add sugars, beat until very creamy, scraping sides of bowl occasionally. Add 2 eggs, one at a time, scraping bowl between each, to incorporate well. Add vanilla. Very gradually beat in flour mixture. Reserve ¾ cup batter; spread remaining batter into prepared baking pan. Sprinkle pecans and white morsels over batter, drizzle with caramel topping. Beat remaining egg and reserved batter together until very light in color. Stir in semisweet morsels. Spread evenly over caramel topping. Bake 35 to 40 minutes or until center is set. Cool completely in pan on wire rack. Remove from pan using foil ends. Cut into squares.

SIMPLY DELICIOUS

County Fair Brownies Makes 12

Blue ribbon good, these are a favorite of mine because of the frosting. To make them into what my world calls the best brownie they know, substitute toffee bits for walnuts in the batter and sprinkle over the frosting. We are lucky to have Brandini Toffee available locally and it is one of the best ever. It is available on-line, expensive but worth it.

2/3 cup unbleached flour
7 tablespoons unsweetened cocoa
½ teaspoon baking powder
½ teaspoon salt
10½ tablespoons unsalted butter

1 cup sugar
1 teaspoon vanilla extract
2 large eggs
2 tablespoons dark corn syrup
1 cup coarsely chopped walnuts

Frosting
2¼ ounces unsweetened baking chocolate
3 tablespoons unsalted butter
1½ cup confectioner's sugar

3 tablespoons hot water
¾ teaspoon vanilla extract
1/3 cup coarsely chopped walnuts or toffee bits

Preheat oven to 350°.
Line 8-inch square pan with parchment paper; butter and flour paper. Sift together flour, cocoa powder, baking powder and salt. Repeat twice. Cream butter with sugar and vanilla until light and fluffy; beat in eggs one at a time; blend in corn syrup. Mix in dry ingredients; stir in walnuts. Pour batter into pan, spread evenly. Bake until tester comes out almost clean, about 30 minutes. Cool. Remove from pan; frost.

Frosting: Melt chocolate and butter in double boiler over simmering water; stir until smooth. Mix in sugar, water and vanilla. Spread frosting over brownie. Sprinkle with walnuts; let stand until frosting is set; this can be expedited by refrigerating for 10 minutes. Cut into squares; serve.

NANCY SCHECHTMAN

What A Surprise Brownies Makes 16

Everywhere, including the store, this is the most requested brownie that I make and one of the easiest to prepare. The surprise is that they have no, nada, non, cholesterol. Start these early enough to chill for ease in cutting otherwise they stick to the knife.

1½ cups sugar
1 cup unbleached flour
¾ cup unsweetened cocoa
1 teaspoon baking powder
¼ teaspoon salt

¾ cup canola oil
4 large egg whites beaten to blend
2 teaspoons vanilla extract
2/3 cup chopped walnuts optional

Preheat oven to 350°.
Grease 8-inch square pan. Combine first 5 ingredients in large bowl. Blend in oil, egg whites and vanilla. Stir in walnuts. Transfer to prepared pan. Bake until brownies are slightly puffed in center and edges are beginning to brown, about 30 minutes. Cover hot brownies in pan with foil; chill overnight or in freezer for an hour. Cut and serve.

Fudgy Brownies

Makes 24-32

For those who love them fudgy they don't come much better than this.

Market in rural Burma (Myanmar)

1 cup unsalted butter
4 ounces chopped unsweetened baking chocolate
2 cups sugar
4 large eggs

1 teaspoon vanilla extract
1 cup unbleached flour
½ teaspoon salt
1 cup chopped walnuts, optional

Preheat oven to 350°.
Lightly grease 13x9-inch baking pan, line with parchment paper. Melt butter and chocolate in microwave until almost melted; stir to combine. Stir in sugar with wooden spoon; beat in eggs one at a time stirring after each addition until eggs are fully incorporated and chocolate mixture is shiny. Stir in vanilla. Add flour and salt; mix until blended. Stir in nuts. Scrape batter into pan. Bake for 30 minutes or until brownies are slightly firm to the touch and a tester indicates the brownies are moist. Let cool completely in pan before cutting.

Gooey Brownies   Makes 32

This is the single item that started my career, business, success and marriage. They were named by my kids who grew up on them. Marty had one at the store before we met and decided it would be worth calling me on the basis of one Gooey. I keep my marshmallows in the freezer; they do not need to be thawed before adding to batter.

4 ounces unsweetened baking chocolate
1 cup unsalted butter
1 cup semisweet chocolate chips
4 large eggs

2 cups sugar
1 teaspoon vanilla extract
1 cup sifted unbleached flour
2 cups miniature marshmallows

Preheat oven to 350°.
Grease and flour 2 9x9-inch pans (for thicker brownies use an 8x8-inch pan as some of my kids do); line pan with foil that hangs over the sides to lift the brownies out without sticking...they really are gooey. Melt together unsweetened chocolate, butter and chocolate chips. Beat eggs until very thick and lemon-colored, the thicker and lighter lemon-colored the better or the brownies will be flat, blend well with chocolate mixture. Mix in sugar, vanilla and flour. Fold in marshmallows. Pour into prepared pans. Bake 30 minutes. Brownies should not be soft but should stick to tester. Cool 10 to 15 minutes. Cut and remove from pan. To make it easier to cut place them in the freezer for 1/2 hour before cutting.

White Chocolate Chunk Brownies

Makes 16

The bridge group is still talking about these.

3 ounces unsweetened baking chocolate
2 cups firmly packed brown sugar
¾ cup unsalted butter
2 large eggs
1 tablespoon vanilla extract

2 cups unbleached flour
2 teaspoons baking powder
½ teaspoon salt
5 ounces white chocolate cut into ¾-inch pieces
¾ cup toasted, coarsely chopped pecans

Preheat oven to 350°.
Grease 9-inch square pan; line bottom with parchment. Melt chocolate and butter in microwave in medium bowl; add sugar, stir to blend well. Cool. Add eggs and vanilla to butter mixture, whisk to combine. Sift together flour, baking powder and salt; add to butter mixture, stir to blend. Stir in white chocolate and pecans. Pour batter into prepared pan. Bake until tester inserted into center comes out almost clean, about 35 minutes. Cool in pan on rack. Run small sharp knife around sides of pan to loosen brownie. Turn onto plate; peel off parchment. Cut and serve.

NANCY SCHECHTMAN

Beyond Decadent Turtle Brownies — Makes 32

My two favorites, chocolate and caramel, in an unbeatable brownie; the caramel gets so gooey that the brownies are difficult to remove from the pan so the pan must be lined with parchment or foil. Serving these in muffin cups keep your platter neat and fingers a bit cleaner. Instead of ice cream topping, use 1 pound bulk caramel melted with ¼ cup of milk.

1½ cups unsalted butter
½ pound unsweetened baking chocolate
6 large eggs
3 cups sugar
1½ cup unbleached flour

1 tablespoon vanilla extract
1 cup chopped pecans
1 16-ounce jar caramel ice cream topping
½ cup chopped pecans
1 cup semisweet chocolate chips

Preheat oven to 350°.
Grease well 2 9-inch square pans, line bottom and sides with parchment or foil; grease again. Melt butter and chocolate together. Beat eggs until very light yellow and foamy; add sugar, beat until thickened. Add chocolate mixture, stir in lightly. Add flour, vanilla and pecans; mix just to moisten flour. Place half batter in prepared pans; bake 20 to 25 minutes. Melt caramels with milk if using. Spread mixture or caramel topping over baked brownies. Sprinkle with ½ cup nuts and chocolate chips. Cover with remainder of batter. Bake an additional 30 minutes. Top will be "gooey". Cool completely before cutting. These can be refrigerated first to aid in cutting.

Oatmeal Carmelitas **Makes 24**
Make plenty, these go fast.

2 cups unbleached flour
2 cups quick cooking, rolled oats
1½ cup firmly packed, brown sugar
1 teaspoon baking soda
½ teaspoon salt

1¼ cup unsalted butter
1 cup semisweet chocolate chips
½ cup chopped, walnuts
1 12-ounce jar caramel ice cream topping
3 tablespoons unbleached flour

Preheat oven to 350°.
Grease 9x13-inch pan. Combine flour, oats, brown sugar, baking soda, salt and butter with mixer at low speed until crumbly. Press half of crumb mixture, about 3 cups, into prepared pan; reserve remaining mixture for topping. Bake 10 minutes. Sprinkle warm base with chocolate chips and nuts. Combine caramel topping and flour; pour evenly over chocolate chips and nuts. Sprinkle with reserved crumbs mixture. Return to oven; bake 18 to 22 minutes or until golden brown. Cool completely before cutting into bars.

Butterfinger Brownies

Easy as pie...actually much easier.

Makes 32

4 ounces unsweetened baking chocolate
¾ cup unsalted butter
2 cups sugar
3 large eggs

2 teaspoons vanilla extract
1 cup unbleached flour
1 cup chopped walnuts
4 coarsely chopped Butterfinger candy bars

Preheat oven to 350°.
Grease 13x9-inch pan. Microwave chocolate and butter in large microwaveable bowl until butter is melted; stir until chocolate is completely melted; stir sugar into chocolate. Mix in eggs and vanilla until well blended. Stir in flour, nuts and Butterfingers. Spread in pan. Bake 30 to 35 minutes or until toothpick inserted in center comes out with fudgy crumbs. Cool in pan before cutting into squares.

U.S. Mints

Makes 16

Silly name, great taste! Allow 4 hours after frosting to cool and serve. Mint chocolate chips can be purchased online at Hershey's chocolate. Cutting the butter and chopping the chocolate make for shorter melting time. You can freeze the butter then grate it, too.

1¼ cups mint chocolate chips
1½ ounces chopped unsweetened baking chocolate
½ cup unsalted butter grated or cut in pieces
½ cup unbleached flour
Pinch salt
1½ teaspoons whipping cream
1½ teaspoons instant espresso powder, optional
½ teaspoon green crème de menthe

3 large eggs
¾ cup sugar
2 tablespoons sugar
Glaze
6 tablespoons mint chocolate chips
½ ounce finely chopped or grated unsweetened baking chocolate
5 tablespoons unsalted butter grated or cut in pieces

Position rack in lowest third of oven; preheat to 350°.
Grease sides of 9-inch square baking pan. Line pan with foil, allowing foil to extend over two sides; grease foil. Melt both chocolates and butter stirring until smooth; cool. Sift flour with salt. Mix cream, espresso powder and crème de menthe. Beat eggs and sugar in large bowl until frothy. Fold in coffee mixture and melted chocolate, then dry ingredients. Spread batter evenly in pan. Bake until toothpick inserted in center comes out with some moist crumbs still attached, about 25 minutes. Gently press down on any raised surfaces to flatten slightly. Cool 30 minutes.

For glaze melt both chocolates and butter in heavy small saucepan over low heat or in microwave, stirring until smooth. Let stand until cool; spread glaze over brownies. Let stand 4 hours at room temperature. Lift brownies from pan using foil sides as aid; fold down foil. Cut into squares.

Coconut Squares

Makes 24-32

I am embarrassed to publish this recipe so that my friends find out how easy they are. They'll be showing up everywhere.

1 cup unsalted butter
½ cup sugar
2 cups unbleached flour

8 ounces shredded coconut
1 14-ounce can sweetened condensed milk
12 ounces semi-sweet chocolate chips

Preheat oven to 350°.
Mix butter, flour and sugar together in food processor only until crumbly. Press into bottom of 9x13-inch pan. Bake 20-25 minutes or just until golden. Do not over-bake as base will crumble. Mix together coconut and condensed milk. Spread evenly on top of baked layer. Return to oven for 20 minutes. Melt chocolate chips; spread to cover coconut. Refrigerate a few minutes to set the chocolate.

Apricot Bars

Makes 16

Apricots, my favorite fruit, these bars are rich and deeply flavored.

Bars in an Israeli street market

2/3 cup dried apricot
½ cup unsalted butter
¼ cup sugar
1 1/3 cups sifted unbleached flour, divided
½ teaspoon baking powder

¼ teaspoon salt
1 cup firmly packed brown sugar
2 well beaten large eggs
½ teaspoon brandy extract, optional
½ cup chopped walnuts

Preheat oven to 350°.
Grease 8-inch square pan. Place apricots in pot with enough water to cover; boil, drain, cook and chop coarsely. Mix butter with sugar and 1 cup flour until crumbly. Press mixture into bottom of prepared pan. Bake 25 minutes. Sift together remaining 1/3 cup flour, baking powder and salt. Beat brown sugar slowly into eggs, beating well after each addition. Stir in flour mixture, flavoring, nuts and apricots. Spread over baked layer. Return to oven; bake 30 minutes longer. Cool in pan before cutting into bars.

Everyone has disasters!

Cake

"Sometimes eating a thick slice of fudge cake with ice cream makes you a better person." Dr. Sun Wolf

Julia Child said that a party without cake is just a meeting.

Although we do love other desserts there is something about a rich, moist slice of cake with a creamy frosting that satisfies one's soul and it's even more fulfilling when it is baked with fresh ingredients in your own kitchen. Not even Costco can top that.

Peppermint Fudge Cake

Serves 12

Chocolate and peppermint is the best combination for me after chocolate and caramel. This production ranks right at the top. It is far from a last minute dessert but each bite is worth every moment of your time. Start early, ideally the day before serving, and be sure to read the whole recipe and check timing before starting.

2 cups unbleached flour
1½ teaspoon baking soda
½ teaspoon salt
1 cup unsweetened cocoa
1 2/3 cup boiling water

1 cup unsalted butter
2 cups sugar
1 ½ teaspoon vanilla extract
3 large eggs

Peppermint Mousse
10 ounces chopped white chocolate
1¾ cup whipping cream

¼ cup sour cream
24 crushed red and white peppermint candies

Ganache
2 cups whipping cream
16 ounces chopped bittersweet or semi-sweet chocolate

Preheat oven to 325°.

Butter and flour three 9-inch cake pans, line with parchment. Blend flour, baking soda and salt. Place cocoa in medium bowl, whisk in boiling water. Cool cocoa mixture to room temperature, whisking occasionally. To cool quickly, place in freezer for 10 minutes. Beat butter in large bowl until very fluffy. Gradually beat in sugar then vanilla and eggs one at a time. At low speed, beat in flour mixture in 3 additions alternating with cocoa mixture in two. Divide batter equally among prepared pans. Bake until tester inserted in center comes out almost clean, about 18 minutes. Cool layers in pans 5 to 10 minutes, turn out onto racks.

Combine white chocolate, ¾ cup whipping cream and sour cream in heavy saucepan. Stir over low heat just until chocolate is melted and smooth. Transfer white chocolate mixture to large bowl; cool to barely lukewarm, whisking occasionally. Mix in candies. Beat remaining 1 cup cream to medium peaks. Fold cream into chocolate mixture in 4 additions. Chill mousse until beginning to set, about 2 hours. Place cake layer on serving plate. Spread half of mousse over top of cake. Top with second layer, remaining mousse and third layer. Chill cake until mousse is cold and set, about 3 hours.

Bring cream to simmer in heavy saucepan; remove from heat. Add chocolate, whisk until melted and smooth. Cool ganache until thick but still pourable, about 45 minutes. Place cake on rack set over baking sheet. Pour ganache over cake, spreading with metal spatula to cover sides evenly. Chill cake until ganache sets, at least 30 minutes and up to 1 day.

NANCY SCHECHTMAN

Nancy's Chocolate Cake was a favorite for birthdays at the store and still is for many of us!

Nancy's Chocolate Cake   Serves 12

This was our signature cake at the shop...with good reason! Does not, surprisingly enough, need refrigeration and will last a week but you'll eat it much sooner.

1 cup unsweetened cocoa
2 cups boiling water
2¾ cups sifted unbleached flour
2 teaspoons baking soda
½ teaspoon salt

½ teaspoon baking powder
1 cup unsalted butter
2½ cups sugar
4 large eggs
1½ teaspoons vanilla extract

Frosting
1 cup semisweet chocolate chips
½ cup light cream

1 cup unsalted butter
2½ cups confectioners' sugar

Filling
1 cup chilled heavy cream
¼ cup confectioners' sugar

1 teaspoon vanilla extract

Preheat oven to 350°.
Grease well and flour 3 9-inch cake pans, line with parchment. Combine cocoa with boiling water; mix with wire whisk until smooth. Cool completely; can be placed in freezer to reduce time. Sift flour with soda, salt and baking powder. At high speed on electric mixer beat butter until very creamy; add sugar, eggs and vanilla beating until light, about 5 minutes. Remember to scrape sides and bottom of bowl occasionally. Beat in flour mixture in fourths, alternating with cocoa in thirds. Do NOT overbeat. Divide evenly into pans gently smooth tops. Bake 20 to 25 minutes or until surface lightly springs back when gently pressed or until there are moist crumbs on a tester. Cool in pans 10 minutes; turn out onto racks. In saucepan combine chocolate, cream and butter stir over low heat until smooth. Or microwave one minute at a time, stirring once, until smooth. Whisk in 2½ cups confectioners' sugar. In bowl set over ice, beat until frosting holds shape. Or place in freezer for 20 minutes and then beat. Whip cream with sugar and vanilla; refrigerate. Place cake layer, top side down on plate, spread with half of cream. Place second layer, top side down spread with rest of cream. Place third layer, top side up. Frost with spatula, sides first, swirling decoratively.

Flourless Chocolate Cake   Serves 8

I like many others but this one was a best seller at the store. It's great for Passover. The cake must be made one day prior to serving! It freezes well for up to one month.

1 cup unsalted butter
1 cup sugar
2 teaspoons vanilla extract
8 ounces melted sweet baking chocolate

8 large egg yolks
8 large egg whites
Grated semisweet baking chocolate

Preheat oven to 350°.
Butter the bottom only of 9-inch spring form pan line with waxed or parchment paper. Beat together butter, sugar, vanilla and chocolate on slow speed. Gradually add egg yolks, one at a time, beating well after each addition. Continue to beat at slow speed for 25 minutes. (I know this sounds tedious but it is well worth it. (It's better if you have a standing mixer, as you can walk away but return to scrape the bowl occasionally.) Beat egg whites until stiff, glossy and holding a peak. Gently fold beaten egg whites into chocolate mixture. Pour ¾ of the mixture into spring form pan. Reserve remaining batter; cover unrefrigerated.

    Bake cake for 20 to 25 minutes until tester inserted in center comes out almost clean. Let stand until completely cooled, cake will sink in the middle, no worries. Remove side of spring form pan. You may leave the cake on the bottom or carefully move off using waxed paper. Spread remaining batter on top; sprinkle with grated semisweet chocolate or chocolate sprinkles. Cover well, refrigerate overnight.

Fudge Chip Pound Cake

Serves 8

Our word? Yummy! Add ice cream and it's even yummier.

6 tablespoons sugar
3 tablespoons unsweetened cocoa
1½ tablespoon water
½ cup unsalted butter
1 cup sugar
2 large eggs
1 teaspoon vanilla extract

1½ cup unbleached flour
1 teaspoon baking powder
¼ teaspoon salt
½ cup milk
½ cup semisweet chocolate chips
1/8 teaspoon baking soda

Preheat oven to 350°.
Butter and flour 9x5-inch loaf pan. Blend sugar and cocoa in heavy saucepan; stir in water. Bring to simmer over medium-low heat, stirring until smooth. Simmer mixture gently 3 minutes. Cool completely. Cream butter until fluffy; gradually beat in sugar until creamy. Beat in eggs one at a time. Blend in vanilla. Sift flour with baking powder and salt. Add to batter alternately with milk, beginning and ending with flour, blending well after each addition. Fold in chocolate chips. Turn ½ batter into prepared pan spreading higher at edges. Divide remaining batter in half. Blend half into cooled cocoa mixture with 1/8 teaspoon baking soda. Spoon over batter in pan, spread leaving ½-inch borders at edges. Cover with remaining batter. Bake until tester inserted in center has soft crumbs, about 45 to 50 minutes. Cool in pan 15 minutes; remove; cool. Dust with confectioners' sugar. Serve.

Apple Cake with Caramel Sauce and Bourbon Whipped Cream

Serves 12

Delish! And so very good in the autumn. I serve it for both Rosh Hashanah and Halloween.

2½ cups sugar, divided
1 tablespoon cinnamon
3 cups unbleached flour
1 tablespoon baking powder
½ teaspoon salt
1 cup canola oil
¾ cup sour cream

Caramel Sauce
1½ cup whipping cream
1 cup packed brown sugar
½ cup dark corn syrup

Bourbon Whipped Cream
3 cups chilled whipping cream
½ cup packed brown sugar
1/3 cup bourbon whiskey

4 large eggs
¼ cup fresh orange juice
2 teaspoons grated orange peel
2 teaspoons vanilla extract
4 cups, about 3 large, cored, peeled and diced Granny Smith apples
1 cup chopped walnuts

¼ cup unsalted butter
1 teaspoon vanilla extract

Preheat oven to 350°.
Butter 12-cup nonstick Bundt pan. Mix ½ cup sugar and cinnamon. Mix flour, baking powder and salt. Whisk remaining 2 cups sugar, oil, sour cream, orange peel, orange juice, eggs and vanilla to blend. Stir in flour mixture. Pour half of batter into pan. Sprinkle half of apples over batter, then half of chopped walnuts and half of cinnamon-sugar mixture; spoon remaining batter over. Sprinkle as before. Bake cake 50 minutes. Cover pan loosely with foil; continue baking until tester inserted near center comes out almost clean. Cool on rack 10 minutes. Turn cake out onto rack; cool completely. Can be made 1 day ahead; cover with cake dome, keep room temperature.

Caramel Sauce: Bring first 4 ingredients to boil in heavy saucepan, stirring occasionally. Reduce heat to medium-high; boil until reduced to 2 cups, stirring occasionally, about 8 minutes. Whisk in vanilla. Cool. To reheat, stir over low heat just until lukewarm.

Bourbon Whipped Cream: Beat cream and sugar in large bowl until soft peaks form. Add bourbon and beat until stiff peaks form. Can be prepared up to 4 hours ahead; cover, refrigerate.

    Dust cake with powdered sugar. Place each piece on plate swirled with warm Caramel Sauce; top with Bourbon Whipped Cream.

Coconut Pound Cake with Lemon Curd Filling — Serves 12

This cake is a beautiful combination of flavor and texture and great for preparing in advance. Remember to cook lemon curd a day in advance. The curd can be used for any recipe and is superb on scones and fresh fruit.

1½ cup unsalted butter
3 cups sugar
6 large eggs
3 cups unbleached flour
¼ teaspoon salt

Orange Glaze
1 cup fresh orange juice
¾ cup sugar

Lemon Curd
6 lemons
2 cups sugar

¼ teaspoon baking soda
1 cup sour cream
4 ounces flaked coconut
2 teaspoons vanilla extract

2 tablespoons fresh lemon juice
1 teaspoon almond extract

¾ cup unsalted butter
6 large beaten eggs

Preheat oven to 300°.
Generously grease 10-inch tube pan with removable bottom; dust with flour. Cream butter; slowly add sugar, beating until very light and fluffy. Beat in eggs 1 at a time. Sift dry ingredients. Blend into butter mixture alternately with sour cream. Mix in coconut and vanilla. Spoon batter into prepared pan; bake until tester inserted in center comes out clean, about 1½ hours. Cool cake in pan on rack 30 minutes. Invert cake onto rack; cool completely. Cake may be baked a day in advance; cover, keep at room temperature. Cut cake in half to make 2 layers using serrated knife. Fill with 1¼ cups lemon curd; spread ¼ cup on top.

Curd: Remove peel from lemons using vegetable peeler, chop finely in processor, or use a very fine zester. Squeeze lemons to measure 1 cup juice. Heat juice with peel, sugar and butter in double boiler over simmering water until sugar dissolves and butter melts. Strain eggs into lemon mixture. Cook until custard leaves a path on back of wooden spoon when finger is drawn across, stirring constantly, about 20 minutes, DO NOT BOIL. Pour into bowl. Place plastic wrap on surface to prevent skin from forming; cool completely. Cover and refrigerate overnight before using; can be refrigerated up to one month.

Glaze: Heat all ingredients in heavy saucepan over low heat, swirling pan occasionally, until sugar dissolves. Increase heat; boil until reduced by ¼, about 5 minutes. Immediately pour glaze over top of cake, allowing some to drizzle down sides.
    Serve passing remaining lemon curd separately.

SIMPLY DELICIOUS

Coconut Cake — Serves 8

Great for birthdays, especially mine! Read ingredients and recipe before beginning. You wouldn't want to throw away the egg whites when separating for the yolks. In a hurry, I've done just that.

3 cups sifted cake flour
2 teaspoons baking powder
¼ teaspoon salt
1 cup unsalted butter
3 cups confectioner's sugar

4 large egg yolks, beaten
1 cup milk
2 teaspoons vanilla extract
1 cup lightly packed shredded coconut
4 large egg whites

Buttercream Frosting
1 cup unsalted butter
8 cups confectioner's sugar
½ cup cream or half and half

1½ tablespoons vanilla extract
Toasted Coconut for Garnish

Preheat oven to 375°.
Sift flour once, measure. Add baking powder and salt. Sift 3 times. Cream butter thoroughly, add sugar gradually. Continue creaming until light and fluffy; add egg yolks beating well. Add flour mixture alternately with milk beginning and ending with flour; beat well scraping sides of bowl after each addition; add coconut and vanilla. Beat egg whites to soft peaks; fold in gently. Bake in two 9-inch round pans for 25 to 30 minutes, until lightly golden and tester inserted comes out almost clean. Cake should be quite moist but not undercooked, just a slight indentation when pressed lightly with your finger. Cool on racks. Frost with buttercream; cover top with toasted coconut.

Frosting: Cream butter until very light and fluffy; add 2 cups sugar, beat until well blended. Add cream, vanilla and remaining sugar beating until thick and smooth and of spreading consistently. Add additional cream if necessary. This will make more butter cream than necessary but less isn't quite enough.

Toasted Coconut: Place a double layer of paper towel on a plate, cover evenly with a cup of coconut. Microwave for one minute; using the paper towels, shake the coconut as the bottom will burn otherwise. Microwave at 30 second intervals, shaking the coconut each time, until it is light brown.

Nemesis au Chocolat   Serves 16

This is a chocolate lover's nemesis, a cross between dense fudge and pudding. The Crème Anglaise is what puts this in the "Killer" category. Serve warm or room temperature. Be certain to allow time for refrigeration of the Crème Anglaise. Cake can be prepared one day in advance; crème Anglaise can be prepared two days in advance.

½ cup water
1½ cup sugar, divided
2 tablespoons vanilla extract
8 ounces finely chopped unsweetened chocolate

4 ounces finely chopped bittersweet or semi-sweet chocolate
1 cup unsalted butter
5 large eggs
Confectioner's sugar

Crème Anglaise
2/3 cup sugar
6 large egg yolks

2 cups milk
1 teaspoon vanilla extract

Preheat oven to 350°.

Grease 9-inch diameter pan; line with parchment paper. Bring 1 cup sugar, ½ cup water and vanilla to boil in heavy saucepan. Remove from heat. Add half of unsweetened and bittersweet chocolates; stir until smooth. Whisk in ½ cup butter. Add remaining chocolate and butter; whisk until smooth. Beat eggs with remaining ½ cup sugar until pale yellow (when you think you are done add another 2 minutes) and a slowly dissolving ribbon forms when beaters are lifted. Beat in chocolate mixture; pour batter into pan. Place cake pan in large baking pan. Add enough boiling water to baking pan to come halfway up side of cake pan. It is safer to add the water after you have the cake on the oven rack. Bake only until cake remains firm in center when shaken, about 30 minutes. Remove from water; cool 10 minutes. Unmold onto plate. Cool completely. Sift confectioners' sugar over cake. Cut into wedges, cake should be very soft. Spoon Crème Anglaise onto plates. Top with cake wedge. Serve.

For Crème Anglaise beat sugar and yolks to blend. Scald milk in heavy saucepan over medium heat, do not allow it to simmer. Gradually beat into yolks. Return to saucepan; stir until mixture has thickened and leaves a path on back of the spoon when finger is drawn across, about 8 minutes; do NOT boil. Strain into bowl. Mix in vanilla. Cool, cover and refrigerate.

Oreo Cheesecake — Serves 12

Prepare one day ahead. Glaze shortly before serving then sit back and wait for the raves.

Crust
1¼ cup graham cracker crumbs
1/3 cup melted unsalted butter
¼ cup firmly packed brown sugar
1 teaspoon cinnamon

Oreo Filling
2 pounds cream cheese
1½ cup sugar, divided
2 tablespoons unbleached flour
4 large eggs
2 large egg yolks
1/3 cup whipping cream
2 teaspoons vanilla extract, divided
1½ cup coarsely chopped Oreos
2 cups sour cream

Fudge Glaze
1 cup whipping cream
8 ounces chopped semisweet chocolate
1 teaspoon vanilla extract
5 Oreos halved crosswise

Preheat oven to 425°.
Blend all crust ingredients in bottom of 10-inch springform pan; press onto bottom and sides. Refrigerate until firm, 30 minutes.

    Beat cream cheese on lowest speed until smooth. Beat in 1¼ cups sugar and flour until well blended. Beat in eggs and yolks until mixture is smooth. Stir in cream and 1 teaspoon vanilla. Pour half of batter into prepared crust. Sprinkle with chopped Oreos. Pour remaining batter over, smoothing with spatula.

Bake 15 minutes. Reduce oven temperature to 225°. Bake 50 minutes, covering top loosely with foil if browning too quickly. Increase oven temperature to 350°. Blend sour cream, remaining 1/4 cup sugar and remaining 1 teaspoon vanilla. Spread over cake. Bake 7 minutes. Refrigerate immediately. Cover with plastic wrap; chill overnight.

Scald whipping cream in heavy saucepan over high heat. Add chocolate and vanilla, stir 1 minute. Remove from heat, stir until melted. Refrigerate glaze 10 minutes.

Set cake on platter, remove spring form. Pour glaze over top of cake. Use a pastry brush to smooth top and sides. Arrange Oreo halves cut side down around outer edge of cake. Refrigerate until ready to serve.

Chocolate Chip Crumb Cake   Serves 16
This snacking cake is good any time of day and is loved by all ages.

Topping
1/3 cup brown sugar
1 tablespoon unbleached flour
2 tablespoons unsalted butter
½ cup chopped pecans
½ cup semisweet chocolate chips

Cake
1¾ cups unbleached flour
1 teaspoon baking powder
1 teaspoon baking soda
¼ teaspoon salt
¾ cup sugar
½ cup unsalted butter
2 teaspoons vanilla extract
3 large eggs
1 cup sour cream
1½ cups semisweet chocolate chips

Preheat oven to 350°.
Topping: Combine brown sugar, flour and butter in small bowl until mixture is crumbly. Stir in nuts and ½ cup chocolate chips.

Grease 13x9-inch baking pan. Combine flour, baking powder, baking soda and salt. Beat sugar, butter and vanilla until creamy. Add eggs, one at a time, beating well after each addition. Gradually add flour mixture alternately with sour cream. Fold in 1½ cups chocolate chips. Spread into pan, sprinkle with topping. Bake 25 to 30 minutes or until toothpick inserted in center comes out clean. Do not over bake. Cool in pan. Cut into squares. Serve warm.

This truck was outside a lunch place we stopped at in Siem Reap, Cambodia. Harry sold some pretty good ice cream!

Desserts

"Bring on the dessert. I think I am about to die." Pierett Brillat-Savarin

"Seize the moment. Remember all those women on the Titanic who waved off the dessert cart." Erma Bombeck

Brownie Pie ala Mode with Foolproof Fudge Sauce   Serves 8

My friend Frank, a connoisseur of all things brownies, ice cream and chocolate sauce, says that this is as good as it gets. Another friend, Sue Swett, spent two years perfecting the sauce. Sauce can be refrigerated a few days but then will become grainy and sugary.

2 ounces unsweetened chocolate
½ cup unsalted butter
1 cup sugar
2 large eggs

¼ cup flour
¼ teaspoon salt
½ teaspoon vanilla extract
¼ cup chopped pecans, optional

Hot Fudge Sauce
¼ cup unsalted butter
¾ cup superfine sugar
1/3 cup evaporated milk

3 ounces unsweetened chocolate
½ teaspoon vanilla extract
Ice Cream

Preheat oven to 350°.
Generously grease 9-inch pie plate with non-stick spray. Melt chocolate and butter in saucepan over low heat or in microwave for 40 seconds, stir until smooth. Add sugar, mix until well combined. Cool to lukewarm. Beat eggs into cooled chocolate mixture with wooden spoon. Add flour, salt, vanilla and nuts. Mix well; pour into prepared pan. Bake for 15 minutes or just until a toothpick inserted comes out almost clean. Do not over bake - it should be moist and fudgy.

Sauce: Melt butter in top of double boiler over gently boiling water. Add sugar and evaporated milk; mix until well combined. Add chocolate. Cover; cook over gently simmering water, 30 minutes. DO NOT stir sauce while cooking. Remove from heat; add vanilla. Beat with wooden spoon until smooth and thick, about 1 minute, keep warm. Serve pie warm or at room temperature with a scoop of ice cream and warm hot fudge sauce. If made in advance, rewarm over gently simmering water; do not microwave as the sauce will become grainy.

Chocolate Mousse   Serves 8

It doesn't come any better than this, originally from the Rib Room in the Royal Orleans. Remember to have eggs room temperature and cream, bowl and beaters well chilled. When folding in egg whites, add ¼ to the chocolate mixture to lighten it. Fold the rest with as few spatula turns as possible, does not need to be fully incorporated. The same is true for the whipped cream. This makes for a feather-light mousse and huge compliments.

3 ounces melted bittersweet chocolate	3 large egg whites
3 ounces melted milk chocolate	2 teaspoons vanilla
¼ cup hot water	2½ tablespoons sugar
3 large egg yolks	1½ cup whipping cream
Pinch salt	Shaved semi-sweet chocolate

Mix chocolates, water, egg yolks, salt and vanilla thoroughly. Beat egg whites and sugar until stiff peaks form. Fold egg whites into chocolate mixture. Whip cream until stiff; fold into chocolate mixture. Decorate with chocolate shavings. Refrigerate to chill until serving, at least one hour.

White and Dark Chocolate Terrine   **Serves 8**

Divinely rich, serve the terrine after a lighter supper. This dessert is worthy of applause. It must be made a day ahead of serving.

White Chocolate Mousse
9 ounces white chocolate broken into small pieces
½ ¼-ounce packet, 1½ teaspoons, unflavored gelatin
5 tablespoons water

Dark Chocolate Mousse
6 ounces semisweet chocolate
¼ cup strong coffee, optional
2/3 ¼ ounce packet, 2 teaspoons, unflavored gelatin

1 tablespoon light corn syrup
2 large egg yolks
2/3 cup whipping cream
2/3 cup sour cream

3 tablespoons water
¼ pound chilled unsalted butter cubed
2 large egg yolks
1¼ cups whipping cream

Line 8x4-inch loaf pan with plastic wrap to overlap edges. Sprinkle gelatin over 2 tablespoons water; let stand 2 to 3 minutes until softened. In saucepan combine remaining water and corn syrup; bring to boil. Remove from heat; stir in gelatin until dissolved. Add white chocolate, beat until chocolate is melted and mixture is smooth. Beat in egg yolks one at a time. Whip whipping cream and sour cream lightly; fold into loaf pan; refrigerate until set. In top of double boiler melt chocolate with coffee; do not use the microwave due to the coffee the chocolate will seize. Sprinkle gelatin over water; let stand 2 to 3 minutes until softened. Set bowl of gelatin in saucepan of hot water; stir until dissolved. Stir gelatin and butter into chocolate mixture; beat until butter has melted and mixture is smooth. Cool; beat in egg yolks. Whip cream lightly to soft peaks, fold into chocolate mixture. Pour dark chocolate mixture over already set white chocolate mousse. Refrigerate until set, cover with overlapping plastic wrap; refrigerate overnight. Unfold plastic wrap from top; turn out onto serving plate. Carefully peel off plastic wrap. Decorate with whipped cream and grated chocolate or sliced strawberries or with raspberries mashed with a bit of balsamic vinegar.

Chocolate Chip Meringues with Ice Cream and Chocolate-Mint Sauce
Serves 8

In the desert I make these in the winter or, when it gets hot, turn the air conditioner cooler so that the meringue stays crisp. In other parts of the country be cautious on very humid days. Hot Fudge Sauce found in the index could be used as well as your favorite jarred sauce. Meringue may be made up to 4 days in advance, store airtight at room temperature. Sauce can be made one day in advance; cover and refrigerate.

Annual Pushkar Camel Fair, India

1 tablespoon melted unsalted butter
½ cup confectioner's sugar
4 large egg whites

1/8 teaspoon salt
2 ounces chopped bittersweet chocolate

Sauce
¼ tablespoon heavy cream
¼ tablespoon water
2 tablespoons sugar

8 ounces chopped bittersweet chocolate
¾ teaspoon peppermint extract
1 pint ice cream

Preheat oven to 225°.
Line 2 heavy baking sheets with parchment. Using small bowl or can as guide, trace 4-inch diameter circles on parchment, turn sheets over. Brush parchment with melted butter. Whisk confectioner's sugar and granulated sugar in small bowl to blend. Using electric mixer, beat egg whites and salt in large bowl on high speed until foamy and beginning to hold soft peaks. Slowly beat in ½ cup sugar continue beating at high speed until whites are stiff and shiny. Fold in remaining sugar, then chocolate. Spoon meringue by generous ½ cupfuls into center of each circle. Use back of spoon to indent center forming shallow bowl. Bake meringues until crisp, about 1½ hours. Place on racks to cool completely. Scoop ice cream into center of meringue; spoon sauce over; serve.

Sauce: Bring cream, water and sugar to boil in medium saucepan over medium heat stirring to dissolve sugar. Reduce heat to low, add chocolate; whisk until melted. Remove from heat; stir in extract. Rewarm sauce over low heat before using.

NANCY SCHECHTMAN

Chocolate-Banana Meringue Torte   Serves 8

This is Keri's, "Mommy, won't you please make it?" favorite to this day. Prepare meringue a day in advance in a cool, dry kitchen. Humidity is the downfall of meringue. This is better assembled a day prior to serving.

Baby banana pod in Panama

3 large egg whites
1 cup sugar
6 ounces semisweet baking chocolate
3 tablespoons water

3 cups chilled whipping cream
¼ cup sugar
3 ripe thinly sliced, bananas

Preheat oven to 400°.
Butter and flour outside bottoms of three 9-inch round pans. Beat egg whites on low speed, one minute. Increase speed to high and continue beating until stiff but not dry peaks form, about 30 seconds. Gradually beat in sugar until glossy, about 1 minute. Spoon onto prepared pans, spreading to within ½-inch of edge. Turn oven off and let meringues stand in oven with door closed at least 8 hours or overnight.

    Melt chocolate with water in double boiler or microwave. Whip cream until soft peaks form. Add ¼ cup sugar; beat until stiff but not dry. Set meringue layer on platter; spread with 1/3 chocolate mixture and ¼ cream. Arrange half of banana slices over cream. Top with second meringue layer, pressing gently; repeat as with first layer. Top with third meringue layer. Frost top and sides of torte with remaining cream; drizzle chocolate over top in decorative pattern. Refrigerate 2 hours before serving.

Viennese Apple Strudel   Serves 8

How many strudel makers are there in the world? That's how many strudel recipes there are. This is still my personal favorite and it's almost as good as the one Marty's mom, Dorothy, made. Ice cream, whipped cream and sabayon are all wonderful accompaniments.

2 slices lightly toasted bread
2 pounds golden delicious apples
2 tablespoons fresh lemon juice
1 tablespoon grated lemon peel
½ cup chopped walnuts
1 cup sugar
¼ cup raisins

1½ teaspoon ground cinnamon
¼ teaspoon ground cloves
¼ teaspoon ground cardamom, optional
¼ teaspoon ground ginger
6 sheets thawed phyllo dough
12 tablespoons melted unsalted butter
Confectioner's sugar

Preheat oven to 350°.
Process bread in processor until crumbs are ground fine. On cookie sheet, bake for 10 to15 minutes until dry and golden; stir occasionally. Cool to room temperature.
    Raise oven temperature to 400°.
    Peel, core and slice apples 1/8-inch thick. Place in bowl with lemon juice and peel, nuts, raisins, ¾ cup sugar and spices; toss until well-blended. Taste, add more sugar if necessary. Brush one sheet phyllo, long side facing you, with butter; sprinkle with 2 tablespoons bread crumbs; repeat with remaining sheets stacking as you go. Spread apple filling on long edge of phyllo; gently roll-up jelly roll fashion. Place seam-side down on baking sheet; brush top with butter. Bake 35 to 45 minutes until golden brown; brushing with butter every 10 minutes. Cool on rack. Sprinkle with confectioner's sugar. Serve warm cut into 1½-inch diagonal pieces.

Plum Galette

Serve 8

Rustic and fresh, galettes are a great ending to a summer supper. Another dessert that is good with ice cream, especially peach! You can substitute one package of puff pastry dough for the pate brisee, I often do.

Pate Brisee
1½ cup unbleached flour
12 tablespoons chilled unsalted butter cut in ½-inch pieces
¼ teaspoon salt
1 cup ice water

Filling
¼ cup sugar
1/3 cup sugar
3 tablespoons ground almonds
3 tablespoons unbleached flour
2½ pounds plums, pitted, cut in ½-inch wedges
3 tablespoons unsalted butter cut in small bits
½ cup apricot preserves strained if necessary

Preheat oven to 400°.
Put flour, butter and salt in food processor; process 5 seconds, butter should still be in pieces. Add ice water; process about 5 seconds longer, just until dough comes together, butter should still be visible in the dough. Remove dough, gather into ball. Wrap in plastic wrap; chill 30 minutes. On lightly floured surface, roll out the dough into 16x18-inch oval 1/16 to 1/8-inch thick. Drape dough over the rolling pin; transfer to large heavy baking sheet. Chill dough until firm, about 20 minutes.

In small bowl, combine ¼ cup sugar with ground almonds and flour. Spread mixture evenly over dough to within 2 inches of edge. Arrange plum wedges on top, dot with bits of butter. Sprinkle all but 1 teaspoon of remaining 1/3 cup of sugar over fruit. Fold dough edges up over plums to create a 2-inch border. If the dough feels cold and firm, wait a few minutes until it softens to prevent from cracking. Sprinkle the border with the reserved 1 teaspoon of sugar. Bake galette in the middle of the oven for 45 minutes to 1 hour until fruit is very soft and crust is richly brown. If any juices have leaked onto baking sheet, slide a knife under the galette to release it from the sheet. Spoon preserves over hot fruit spread evenly with a pastry brush onto crust for a beautiful glazed finish. Cool galette to room temperature before serving.

Fresh Blackberry Tart with Walnut Streusel and Vanilla Ice Cream

Serves 8

This tart is delicious served warm with full fat ice cream. You may substitute peaches, nectarines, apricots or raspberries. My family, to a person, loves this tart.

8 sheets phyllo dough
½ cup melted unsalted butter
½ cup sugar
½ cup gingersnap cookie crumbs
4 tablespoons chilled unsalted butter
½ cup unbleached flour
½ cup sugar

½ cup toasted coarsely chopped walnuts
1 tablespoon fresh lemon juice
1/3 cup sugar
2 tablespoons cornstarch
1/8 teaspoon ground nutmeg
3 cups fresh blackberries

Line large baking sheet with parchment paper or aluminum foil. Lay 1 sheet phyllo lengthwise on baking sheet. Lightly butter phyllo working from edge toward center; sprinkle with 1 tablespoon sugar and 1 tablespoon cookie crumbs. Repeat. Repeat with third sheet but place crosswise over first two sheets. Layer fourth sheet over third; repeat with fifth sheet laying diagonally over stack. Lay sixth sheet on stack on opposite diagonal forming an X with the fifth. Lay 7 the same as 5 buttering and sprinkling each sheet as you go. Lay 8 the same as 6. Give final buttering and sprinkling. Roll edges toward center, creating 8-inch tart shell with 1-inch rim. Lightly butter shell, generously sprinkle bottom and rim with sugar. Refrigerate shell to harden butter.

Preheat oven to 400°.
Combine flour and sugar in processor. Add chilled butter, pulse until mixture resembles small peas. Chill streusel. Toss chilled streusel with walnuts. Stir together lemon juice, sugar, cornstarch and nutmeg. Toss fruit with mixture spoon into tart shell. Top with walnut streusel. Bake tart until berries are bubbling and shell is crisp and golden brown, 25 to 30 minutes. If shell seems to be browning too quickly, cover with aluminum foil and continue baking until filling is cooked through. Transfer to wire rack, cool; cut into wedges with serrated knife. Serve warm with ice cream.

Blueberry Crisp   Serves 8

A simple, fresh summer treat this is also wonderful with mixed berries and you can add peaches, too.

3 cups blueberries
¼ teaspoon fresh lemon juice
½ cup sugar
1/3 cup unbleached flour

1 teaspoon cinnamon
¼ teaspoon ground ginger
2 tablespoons melted unsalted butter
Your favorite ice cream

Preheat oven to 400°.
Gently mix berries with lemon juice; spread in greased 8 or 9-inch pie pan. Mix sugar, flour, cinnamon and ginger. Add butter; toss with fork until mixture is crumbly. Sprinkle over berries. Bake 20 minutes or until topping is lightly browned. Cool about 10 minutes or until topping is crisp. Spoon over scoops of ice cream and dig in.

Flaming Bananas over Ice Cream   Serves 4

Wonderfully simple, yet very dramatic. Vanilla can be substituted for rum although it will not ignite.

1/3 cup shredded coconut
1/3 cup chopped pecans
¼ cup packed brown sugar
1 teaspoon grated orange peel

¼ cup unsalted butter
4 sliced firm ripe bananas
4 tablespoons dark rum, divided
1 pint butter pecan or vanilla ice cream

Combine first 4 ingredients. Melt butter in heavy skillet over low heat; add bananas. Sprinkle with coconut mixture. Add 2 tablespoons rum. Cook until bananas are tender, stirring occasionally, about 3 minutes. Tilt skillet. Add remaining rum. Heat slightly; ignite with match. Scoop ice cream into bowls. When flames subside spoon bananas and sauce over ice cream. Serve immediately.

Fresh Strawberries and Balsamic Sabayon   Serves 6
Wonderful with pound cake, ice cream, on their own or anything you can imagine.

¼ cup packed brown sugar
¼ cup water
4 large egg yolks
3 tablespoons balsamic vinegar

½ cup chilled whipping cream
2½ baskets hulled and quartered strawberries
2 tablespoons sugar

Combine first 3 ingredients and 2 tablespoons vinegar in stainless steel bowl. Set bowl over pan of simmering water; do not allow bowl to touch water; whisk until sabayon triples in volume, thermometer should register 160°, about 4 minutes. Place bowl over larger bowl filled with ice and water whisk sabayon until cool. Beat cream in another medium bowl to soft peaks. Add sabayon and fold together. Cover and refrigerate. Puree ¾ cup berries with 2 tablespoons sugar and remaining 1 tablespoon balsamic vinegar in processor. Pour puree into large glass bowl. Add remaining berries, toss to coat. Serve strawberries on top of thin slices of cake with sabayon on the side.

Sautéed Apple Slices with Apricot Sauce   Serves 6
So easy and sooo good.

Fruit sales lady, Floating Market, Bangkok

3 ounces dried apricots
2 16-ounce cans apricot halves drained
3 cored, thinly sliced Granny Smith apples

1/3 cup sugar
1 teaspoon vanilla extract
1 pint vanilla ice cream

Place dried apricots in bowl, cover with boiling water. Let stand 10 minutes; drain thoroughly. Puree dried apricots in food processor 10 seconds. Add canned apricots, blend 20 seconds. With machine running add ¼ cup water; mix well, puree should be thick but flowing, add more water if necessary. Transfer to container; cover tightly. Cool until 15 minutes before serving. Combine apple slices, sugar and vanilla in large skillet. Place over high heat; cook, tossing mixture until apples are tender but still crisp, about 3 minutes. Spoon sauce onto each plate; top with scoop of ice cream. Arrange warm apple slices on ice cream. Serve immediately.

Peking Apples   **Serves 4**

A mildly extravagant ending to any dinner, especially one that is Asian.

1 large egg
½ cup water
1 cup unbleached flour

4 peeled, cored, thickly sliced Granny Smith apples
2½ cups canola oil

Syrup
1 tablespoon canola oil
2 tablespoons water
6 tablespoons packed light brown sugar

2 tablespoons light corn syrup
Ice cold water

Stir egg and water into flour to make thick batter. Dip each apple slice in batter to evenly coat, allow excess to drain off. Heat oil in wok until smoking; add apple pieces in small batches; deep-fry 3 minutes until golden brown. Using slotted spoon, remove to paper towels drain. In small saucepan, gently heat oil, water and sugar, stir until sugar has dissolved. Simmer 5 minutes, stirring. Stir in corn syrup; boil 5 to 10 minutes until thick and syrupy. Reduce heat to very low. Dip each piece of apple into syrup to coat, then place in ice water a few seconds. Remove to serving dish. Repeat with remaining apples.

Fried Bananas   **Serves 4**

Asians rarely serve baked goods for dessert which makes these bananas so ideal.

4 cups unsalted butter
½ teaspoon baking soda
Pinch sea salt
2 tablespoons sugar
1 large egg
6 tablespoons water

2 tablespoons shredded coconut
4 firm bananas
4 cups canola oil
Fresh mint for garnish
2 tablespoons honey

Sift flour, baking soda and salt into bowl. Stir in sugar. Whisk in egg, add enough water to make very thin batter. Whisk in coconut. Peel bananas. Cut in half lengthways, then crosswise. Heat oil in wok; dip banana in batter, deep-fry in batches until golden, do not crowd. Remove; drain on paper towel. Garnish with mint or lychees. Serve immediately passing honey separately.

Loving his first cone at the park.

Ice Cream Pie with Variations

"Ice cream is exquisite. What a pity it isn't illegal." Voltaire

"I doubt whether the world holds for anyone a more soul-stirring surprise than the first adventure with ice cream." Heywood Braun

Don't wait for summer; I make these all year long. When asked for the recipe, which happens often with these, I tell people to use their imagination and then I am asked to bring one or two along. So what I present here are suggestions to expand your imagination. When I make two I use different flavors and toppings to provide options for guests.

NANCY SCHECHTMAN

These are definitely easier than pie and really fun to create. Use your favorite flavors and remember that the list below is merely suggestion. Start early to allow for freezer time. The advantage to using Oreos is that the creamy inside helps to hold the crust together, only use regular as double stuffs are just too much.

Serves 8

22 crushed Oreo cookies
¼ cup melted unsalted butter
2 pints different flavored ice cream
Gingersnap cookies
Chocolate wafers
Graham crackers
Vanilla wafer
Your favorite cookie

1 12-ounce jar fudge sauce
1 12-ounce jar chocolate mint sauce
1 12-ounce jar marshmallow crème
1 12-ounce jar caramel sauce
1 12-ounce jar butterscotch sauce

Semisweet chocolate chips
Semisweet mini chocolate chips
Heath chips
Crushed candy bars
Swirled white and dark chocolate chips
Chopped nuts
Colored or chocolate sprinkles
Miniature marshmallows
Toasted shredded coconut

Crush Oreos or other cookie in processor. Add butter; process until well blended. Press onto bottom and sides of 9-inch glass pie plate. Freeze 30 minutes. Spread one pint of softened ice cream over crust. Freeze 1 hour. Cover with compatible sauce, sprinkle with nuts, candy, marshmallows or whatever suits your fancy. Freeze until solid, at least one hour. Top with second pint of softened ice cream. Again freeze then spread with second topping and sprinkle with, toasted coconut, mini chips, sprinkles, or your own concoction. Freeze. Allow to soften just a bit before serving to facilitate cutting.

Buttered Nut and Rum Sauce — Servings: 8

Deceptively delicious drizzled over ice cream, baked or sautéed fruit, crepes or pound cake.

2/3 cup chunky peanut butter
2/3 cup light corn syrup
1/4 cup rum or brandy
Stir ingredients together until well blended.

Hot Fudge Sauce — Servings: 8

The only trick to this is patience. Created by Susan Swett, it is simply the best! The sauce can be refrigerated a few days but will then become grainy. Warm over simmering water before serving over your favorite ice cream or eat it straight from the spoon.

¼ cup unsalted butter
¾ cup superfine sugar
1/3 cup evaporated milk

3 ounces unsweetened baking chocolate
1 teaspoon vanilla extract

Melt butter in top of double boiler over gently boiling water. Add sugar and evaporated milk; stir well until combined. Add chocolate. Cover; cook over gently simmering water 30 minutes. DO NOT stir while cooking. Remove from heat; add vanilla. Beat with wooden spoon until smooth and thick, about 1 minute. Keep warm to serve.

Conversion Table

3 Teaspoons	=	1 Tablespoon
2 Tablespoons	=	1 Liquid Ounce
4 Tablespoons	=	¼ Cup
1 pint	=	2 Cups
1 Quart	=	4 Cups
1 Fluid Ounce	=	2 Tablespoons
8 Fluid Ounces	=	1 Cup
16 Fluid Ounces	=	1 Pint or 2 Cups
1 Pound Butter	=	2 Cups (4 Sticks)

Ingredient Conversions

½ Tablespoon Cornstarch	=	1 Tablespoon Flour
1 Cup Cake Flour	=	7/8 Cup Sifted All-Purpose Flour
1 Cup Corn Syrup	=	1 Cup Sugar plus 1 Cup Water
1 Ounce Chocolate	=	3 Tablespoons Cocoas plus 1 Tablespoon Butter
1 Cup Heavy Cream	=	1/3 Cup butter plus ¾ Cup Milk (but will not work for whipping)
1 Cup Buttermilk	=	1 Cup Milk plus 1 Tablespoon Lemon Juice or Vinegar
¼ Cup Chopped Fresh Herbs	=	1 Tablespoon Dried Herbs
1 Teaspoon Chopped Herbs	=	¼ Teaspoon Dried Herbs
1 Cup Grated Cheese	=	¼ Pound

Interesting Information

Baking powder and baking soda are both chemical leaveners.

- Baking soda, when combined with an acidic ingredient releases carbon dioxide, which forms into bubbles in the food which, when heated, expand and help to rise or lighten the final product.
- Baking powder is a mixture of baking soda and an acid that, combined in liquid, create the same reaction.
- Recipes that call for both baking powder and baking soda usually also contain an acid ingredient such as vinegar, buttermilk, molasses, lemon juice, sour cream, honey or chocolate.
- Baking powder cannot be substituted for baking soda due to its acidic reaction which will affect flavor, texture and color.

Bees have been kept for honey since the time of the Ancient Egyptians, and probably before. It was valuable enough to be used as currency and given as a tribute to a conqueror.

Sugar cane first grew in Polynesia spreading to India and Persia.

- The Arabs grew sugar cane at the end of the 11th century. The Crusaders brought sugar to Europe.
- Sugar was a rare luxury in the Middle Ages so honey was more commonly used in cooking.
- It was the end of the 15th century when sugar cane was taken to the New World.
- Sugar was first made from sugar beet, versus cane, in the 18th century.

What would a baker be without vanilla?

- Vanilla is the second most expensive spice in the world after saffron because growing the vanilla seed pods is labor-intensive as is harvesting saffron.
- Cheaper synthetic vanillas do not have the pure, spicy, delicate flavor and the peculiar bouquet.
- Vanilla was once so rare and expensive that only royalty had access to it.
- At one time vanilla was considered an aphrodisiac.
- Vanilla is the fruit of a thick green orchid vine that grows on the edge of the Mexican rain forests. The Aztecs developed the fermentation process using vanilla to flavor their cocoa drink "xocolatl". It is a thicker, darker bean than others that has a smooth, strong, rich fragrance and flavor. The problem is that Mexican manufacturers add coumarin that is banned by the FDA. Purchase Mexican vanilla only from reputable suppliers.
- Today 70-80% of vanilla comes from the islands of Madagascar and Reunion in the Indian Ocean where the plants were introduced around 1840. These beans have a smooth, rich, sweet flavor. Tahitian beans add subtle flavor and bold aroma to lighter desserts. When using the whole vanilla bean the complexity of flavors and aromas of the bean are released. In custards, milk, cream, syrups and other liquids they impart a wonderful flavor and their small dark seeds add dimension to your dessert. Tahitian beans are more expensive as the bean is about twice the size of those from other areas.
- Never bother with dried out beans found in the spice sections of groceries. They are past their prime and not worth the money. Buy vanilla beans from a spice shop or on-line.
- Always look for beans that are shiny and black, tender, plump and moist. Use them immediately.
- To use, cut beans in half lengthwise and scrape out seeds and pulp. Add this, along with the pod, to your liquid and steep.
- One whole vanilla bean equals 2 to 3 teaspoons of vanilla extract.

INDEX

Apple
Apple Cake with Caramel Sauce and Bourbon Cream, 40
Peking Apples, 59
Sautéed Apples with Apricot Sauce, 58
Viennese Apple Strudel, 54

Apricot
Apricot Bars, 30
Apricot Buttons, 7
Lemon Thumbprint Cookies, 8
Sautéed Apples with Apricot Sauce, 58

Banana
Flaming Bananas over Ice Cream, 57
Fried Bananas, 60
Chocolate-Banana Meringue Torte, 53

Berries
Blueberry Crisp, 57
Fresh Blackberry Tart with Walnut Streusel, 56
Fresh Strawberries and Balsamic Sabayon, 58

Caramel
Beyond Decadent Turtle Brownies, 25
Oatmeal Carmelitas, 26
OMG Brownies, 19

Chocolate
Beyond Decadent Turtle Brownies, 25
Brownie Pie a la Mode, 49
Fudgy Brownies, 22
Butterfinger Brownies, 27
Chocolate Mint Sugar Drops, 13
Chocolate Mousse, 50
Chocolate-Banana Meringue Torte, 53
Chocolate-filled Thumbprint cookies, 16
County Fair Brownies, 20
Fantasy Fudge Cookies, 13
Hot Fudge Sauce, 63
Flourless chocolate Cake, 37
Fudge Chip Pound Cake, 38
Gooey Brownies, 23
Island Treasure Cookies, 17
Mint Chocolate Cookies, 15

NANCY SCHECHTMAN

Nancy's Chocolate Cake, 36
Nemesis au Chocolat, 44
Oatmeal Carmelitas, 26
OMG Brownies, 19
Oreo Cheesecake, 45
Peppermint Fudge Cake, 33
Triple Chocolate Cookies, 6
U. S. Mints, 28
What A Surprise Brownies, 21
White and Dark Chocolate Terrine, 51
White Chocolate Chunk Brownies, 36

Coconut
Coconut Cake, 43
Coconut Macaroons, 11
Coconut Pound Cake with Lemon Curd Filling, 41
Coconut Squares, 29
Island Treasure Cookies, 14

Ice Cream
Blackberry Tart with Walnut Streusel, 56
Blueberry Crisp, 57
Brownie Pie a la Mode, 49
Buttered Nut Rum Sauce, 62
Flaming Bananas over Ice Cream, 57
Hot Fudge Sauce, 62
Ice Cream Pie, 61
Sautéed Apples with Apricot Sauce, 58

Lemon
Coconut Pound Cake with Lemon Curd Filling, 41
Lemon Thumbprint Cookies, 8

Oatmeal
Chew Oatmeal Toffee Crunch Cookies, 4
Oatmeal Carmelitas, 26

Peppermint
Mint Chocolate Cookies, 15
Peppermint Fudge Cake, 33

Peanut Butter
Buttered Nut Rum Sauce, 62
Decadent Peanut Butter Chocolate Chip Cookies, 14

Pecans
Beyond Decadent Turtle Brownies, 25
OMG Brownies, 19

Walnuts
Apricot Bars, 30
Apricot Buttons, 7
Fudgy Brownies, 22
Butterfinger Brownies, 27
County Fair Brownies, 20
Triple Chocolate Cookies, 6
Walnut Lace Cookies, 5
What A Surprise Brownies, 21
White Chocolate
White Chocolate Chunk Brownies, 36
White Chocolate Haystacks, 14
White and Dark Chocolate Terrine, 51

Having tea and sweets in a Berber woman's home, Morocco

Thank You

To Kathi Barnett who convinced me to sell the Gooey Brownies
To Stacy whose help has been invaluable and Kenny for editing
To Keri and Kenny whose holiday cookies were unique, for their help baking and for their love
To my customers at Nancy's who allowed me to experiment on them and returned for more
To my Cookie Monsters near and far
To my 6:00 a.m. friends who smile when I appear with a pan in hand
To Mom who swears she doesn't eat sweets but gobbles whatever I bake
To Kathi whose faith keeps me going daily
To Les who knows why
To Marty who swears to anyone who'll listen that my biscotti and baklava are the best and who is the absolute love of my life

Made in the USA
San Bernardino, CA
05 November 2015